EVERYWHERE WEST

EVERYWHERE WEST

poems by Chris Green

Mayapple Press, 2019

Published by   Mayapple Press
                362 Chestnut Hill Road
                Woodstock, NY 12498
                mayapplepress.com

ISBN 978-1-936419-88-3
Library of Congress Control Number 2019930227

ACKNOWLEDGEMENTS

Many of the poems in this collection have appeared in the following publications: *Atticus Review, Court Green, Fifth Wednesday Journal, Miramar, Poetry East, Prairie Schooner, Poet Lore, Quiddity, RATTLE, Tampa Review,* and *The Eloquent Poem: An Anthology of Form Poems.*

For Lexa, Callie & Lydie

Cover design by Judith Kerman; cover art by Natalie Bontumasi; cover photo by Mark Neumann. Photo of author by Calliope Green. Book designed and typeset by Judith Kerman with titles in Butler Stencil and text in Adobe Garamond Pro.

Contents

What is fate but the density of childhood?
—Rainer Maria Rilke

The Life

Small things in this world are mine.
My daughters, two ungrown girls,
perfect in substance like lightning
and sea are carrying on.
Today, they play salon
and call their place, "The Life."
One wraps a sopping towel on my head.
Her sister lotions my feet.
I have a choice of hairdo:
The Ocean or The Prince.
Such pageants are when I bid farewell
to non-existence,
when a girl with my eyes
and in kindness gives me The Ocean
with her mother's comb.
The life under this roof,
where all joy and fears stem from:
women and babies and men.

The Leaf

Leaves are everyone's metaphors for death, but there I was
at the beginning of my marriage.
Lexa had a new job and I was walking the streets thinking how she sticks
        with things
and how my endless confusion and other issues were maybe killing us.
But we were younger, and nothing seemed deathlike. She was solving things.
I was out there walking down the block.
This will sound like an overtly poetic predicament,
but in that moment I saw an overly large leaf on the sidewalk. And so did
the man walking toward me. There is no such thing as integrity—
we both dove. We wrestled and rolled.
People stopped and tried to understand.
Finally, I called out, "I'm a poet!" Meaning, I wrestle professionally.
Meaning, my relationship with all things is perfect and ancient.
Suddenly, he hissed, "Let go, or I'll tear!"
He tore.

And so, I was there (or I am here)
gripping the merest fraction of what he stole.

Memory with Reality in It

History is memories hot and cold. I remember standing in front of my first apartment when, very slowly, my grandmother drove by. She was in her gold Honda looking around, confused, trying to find . . . me? I didn't move. This memory has always sat strangely. Like Joyce says, "Paralysis." All of my boyhood lost, something uncanny about how I stood as witness. That day she was distant from home, and it was not long before she died alone in Uncle Mike's condominium.

The Broken Hawk

in memory of Gary Solis

With uncles (look close-up) most are gloomy
or in their sad histories quite human,
but occasionally you'll look at someone like Gary who, it's said,
was an angel in our worn family.
In this picture he is wild with kindness, always in the woods or mud,
a gentle boy of the fifties bent over searching the creaking forest
and lonely fields.

He was naïve enough and once pressed a cloth
to a crippled hawk who never smiled.
There was the old house, the patchwork of flowers, the washed clothes
on the line.
He cared for little stricken things . . . anything from the blue earth.
I believe he told the bird it would never die.
The whole of that year his small, blistered hands tended to the harsh body.
You can't repair a wing.
But he perceived nothing completely.

By fall the hawk was something deadly again.
In a firm wind, it flapped a curve across the mountain,
left him in a blaze of darkness unpacified, thankless.

Clouds Assemble Vaguely

It's best to imitate the dying in poems,
line by line, the gazelle's head in the lion's mouth.

And you are calm like August, yet can't see the morning
in front of your face. That's what you tell the doctors.

The MRI's faint wash of color like a sunset
that worries. Clouds assemble vaguely.

In silence, you imagine a thousand years ago
when you lived resolutely in the fleshy world. To think,

last week you picked up a novella by Suskind about a man
terrified by a pigeon. These days, you cry or cry out.

Your corpuscles like magpies in the fields, their
collective unorderliness. You'd rather consider the festivities

of summer—the quiet of blue skies, undisciplined
mosquitoes, and nights shrill with crickets.

Others are dreaming or picking their noses.
Obliviousness is what you miss, and this feeling

is continuous and teasing. You rise at sunup.
Surprised by the actual gold, you count everything you have:

fire, shadows, sweet songs, sex, walks, idiocy, sorrow, bright stars.
Not art, but fact—your daughter's accumulated glow

is more blinding than the imagination needs. You watch
as she lights and leaves the room singing.

Since life is deadly, this morning you remember Africa
where thousands of flamingos like pink flames

ring a lake above which dark eagles wait.
The ultrasonic image from the hospital, which

you stack with bills in the hall, appears to be
a pure white doe in morning fog. Like everything,

she is a blurred form (tries not to be seen)
and is thinking the usual things.

A Vision of Now

Lydie at the dinner table, the prophet of what is not talked about:
"When I grow up, I'm going to be a nonalcoholic."

She gives me a jump-start. Here we are, here I am tonight,
a kind of pitiful dream come true.

How comforting to slip into the mode of triumphant drunk.
I feel Lydie's warning signs, her grave

little poet's heart; sometimes her omens are abandoned on the floor:
Good morning. Welcome to the dragon's lair.

And her glimpses of anguish in the bathtub, the time she grabbed her doll
        by the hair:
"Hi Barbie, do you like the drink without poison that I gave you?"

How she seeks clarity.
When I think of her, whatever evil in my body, I feel no pain.

The Daughter

She'd rather curse than cry: the raw daughter of uncontrolled, traditional tantrums (not the paper-doll daughter of Lear); the daughter of Sappho, blooming and profligate as every daughter; the daughter skipping rope, blonde legs kicking; the daughter whose sin is flesh; the daughter as she appears in Baptist hymns; the daughter of Otomo, a gem in her comb box shaped by the god of the sea; the daughter drawing an inscrutable house in crayon; the ancient daughter whose boredom is stone; the daughter looking at me with the eyes of a lion; the actual daughter I call Memory; the daughter, who like an arrow, found us in suffering and joy; the moony daughter who is the cool white air; Hugo's daughter, whose death was endless and sudden; the heretic daughter and her sharp truth discovered; the daughter who is entering loneliness; the daughter Yeats imprisoned under a poem; Plath's daughter, guileless and clear, instructed to wait behind great desks; the lyric daughter no one can save, the child of untrained perfect language; these daughters are no dearer than the daughter waiting, patient and grave, waving "come closer" in the dark hour of change.

Praise Poem

after Lucille Clifton's "Praise Song"

to my daughter callie
who loped into the road,
from the grass into the street one sunday morning.
she was five.   Praise to the car
who stopped in time.
Praise to her who understood little to nothing
of what had happened.
the air welcomed her back without judgement.
like all children, she saw something on the other side.
Praise to getting from here to there.
so there she was, lightly in her bones,
and i, forced to swallow.
she came back waving as if from a new shore.

Death of the Guinea Pig

In the corner of the yard,
all of us gathered. The little scene etched there:

my daughter, solemn,
bent over the hole in sorrow,

the first she had ever known.

George was someone like all of us—
a squirrel of sorts, a guy on the run.

He did not inhabit the world of dollars,
ammunition, games of logic.

He was a thing without treachery,

a soft target
in the wilderness of the dead.

The Day's Story

Outside it was the rusted green Oldsmobile beside
our sagging fence. The sun austere,
early morning cold and cloudless.
He dragged himself out the door like a crow
off to another world. How I missed him.
It was immediate and deep.
I am three, my father passing through the needle's eye.
I stood alone, gripped Mom.
I stared at him waving at me.
These moments within memory, silent
prayers at sea.

The Poem as Dog

Our first house next to the railroad tracks,
I was the reason we were all there.
My father elsewhere in leather gloves
in love with his paycheck. And my mother
like a window or the color blue,
waiting for him. And the huge dog
who, at the cry of a train, would whimper
and hide beneath the kitchen table—
her broad back lifting it off the floor.
This is exactly as I knew it would be.
Not yet the spoiled, rude, wasteful boy,
the first son casting shadows. I sat
with the dog and talked, but the talk was
stroking her warm fur. I watched Mom smoke.
I couldn't speak it. I would close my eyes—
the house and all the wood that shook,
and the dog bellied down and broken.
We endured. We lolled between the hell
of trains, her head against mine.
Shivering, she did not raise her eyes.
My father was news from the outside.
I could not stop him from coming home.

Mother's Room

Today she happens to be gone.
I reach out and flick on the light.
This evening in Utah the house is bleeding;
wherever I look
she has bought every knick knack.
The sad ceramics
of her clowns stained with dull suffering,
the yellow scars of stuffed bears
wounded by years.
She has jumbled species, made some sense,
some world out of pigs and baskets,
toothpicks and cats, a crystal bull, for instance.
I look around the room
remember being a child in the dark.
I've caused her a great many worries.
We are the empty birdcage:
she was forced to marry, pregnant with me.
And the starved wooden friar
bent over a chessboard is my father's affair,
which has lasted twenty years.
Look there. Huddled alone, gripped in cold,
Mother is a Mexican figurine.
She kneels, silently raving,
chest up, and refuses to move.
My presence makes her pray.

Now that I Am Forever a Child

It only takes one night to realize how forbidding
and unnatural one's life can be.
How suddenly I realized they'd never touched in front of me.
It was the hour
of my threadbare mother,
their marriage already dead.
I knew this as a boy.
That night inside the restaurant's
gold and oak, I finally spoke.
He was frightened and fighting and cursing.
I said, "Tell her she is beautiful."
He looked lost,
or was looking for something lost.
I said, "Kiss her."
It would have made more sense to ask,
"Can you work all day and not drink at all?"
He said, "You want a kiss!"
and dropped his lips
on her mouth like a fist.
It was obscene, aggressive and long.
I was transfixed; my heart straining.
When he finished, he said, "There, are we happy?"
Which is to say, his face was punitive red,
and only time would change him.

Morning Sky

Morning sky: again: day after day but today is breakthrough day
—*from James Schuyler's "The Morning of the Poem"*

THE FIRST POEM IN THE WORLD

The nonsense of nature is everywhere beneath the sky.
I remember once my dad kicked me hard & high
into a gorgeous Utah morning. His leg kept going up and up
(he was a professional punter of sons). There was soaring
& I was floating over the Salt Lake valley—
I found you could live quietly.
Summer lay teeming underneath, the gardens, the over-ripe flowers,
the yellows & dark greens . . .
I was part of the great balanced sky.
The brightness kept coming on, the bleached outline
of the Wasatch Mountains, & an impulse to stay.
In all my innocence, I watched the world
trying to learn the lesson of it. Like some pre-adolescent Beckett,
it always seemed to me I died young,
& that my body bore it out. But that morning, alone in the early sun,
I had the feeling I'd grow older than the day.

THANKS

Today I look at the sky
& remember a friend's funeral.
Merwin says, "after funerals
we are saying thank you
after the news of the dead
whether or not we knew them
we are saying thank you."

The nature of nature:
it's a fact a warthog is faster than a lion,
but (& this is important)
he is quite forgetful.
A warthog chased by a lion

will forget why he is running,
suddenly stop
to taste delicious grass tips . . .
kneel on his wrists
to say thanks.

EARLY LIFE

When Lydie was three, she said
her favorite bird was a breathing bird.
Now she reads this poem about my death
and says it needs more rhyme.

I'm up early, everyone
asleep but Lydie & me.
We write together at the kitchen table.
The tilt of her head & the pen,
her curved fingers,
telegraph the movements of earth.
Maybe we're living parallel
to each other & part of a whole.
I don't know.

At seven, she's writing a song:
"The First Thing You Die for Is Love."

I stare at her
as if she were a road somewhere—
seven little miles unwind,
already level & long.

WHEREVER PRINCE IS

I read that the film *Purple Rain* cured Eric Clapton of depression.
In the moment I write this, my lovely, rebellious daughter Callie
won't accept that Prince is dead. If she hears any mention of him,
she'll say something like, "How do we know he's really gone?"
She claims at worst he's in a coma, a machine pumping his blood.
I try to convince her, but my heart's not in it. My audience is just a kid.
Death is a pretty poor excuse for children. She says, "In my opinion,
Prince is worn out. But I guess he goes on somehow."

Lullaby

The winds are high
    & the girls practice
their music
    at the same time.
Callie plays "Silent Night"
    on the piano.
Lydie sings "Ring of Fire"
    on her ukulele.
Their duet a furious
    headache, a disturbing dream—
children who keep appearing
    one a flower,
one a flame.
    The truest song
ever heard. The discord.
    The daily joy
of just simply being.
    Bewildered, I
sit at the kitchen table
    & the dog drinks
a round from the toilet.

The Father Commanding No

Callie says, "Whenever I see a shooting star,
I always wish for the same thing:
For safety throughout the world.
Even though what I really want is a hedgehog."

You would think kids live without the frills of philosophy,
but one of their greatest pleasures is showing us
to be old pricks.
It's her beginner's mind vs. my flooded one.

To lighten our face-offs,
she says her favorite word is "bubble"
because there's no mean way to say it.
Try it. "Bubble!"

DAUGHTER RIGHT IN MY EAR

Lydie plays her ukulele—"Johnny Comes Marching Home Again."
She sits across from me at the kitchen table.
I'm happy. Are we happy?
Lydie is at the beginning. It gets difficult. The right song is the right
        question.

The other day I tried to get her interested in reading the *New York Times*.
She tried for a few seconds & said, "Newspapers are boring.
They're only good for art projects." She was right, but I kept reading
because I'm tired, tired of playing such things as family where she insists
we can be any age & it's boring. For instance, once I was the daughter
& she was my age
& she sat there reading while I sat there waiting for the day when we
could each go do whatever we're going to do. What was it she said
        yesterday?
I hold many grudges.

Nevertheless, the scene at our table is unquiet & has a theme.
& this thing is not abstract. & her singing is midair. Now
"Yellow Rose of Texas." Next "She'll Be Coming 'Round the Mountain."

DEGREES OF BREATHING

Inhale think peace, exhale think calm
& on & on . . .

Maybe we're alright.
But the skull is a busy place—
something the kids made up:

What is the opposite of good?
Donald Trump.

DARK WORLD

The yogi says—
"Flex the space
between your anus

& your genitalia
enthusiastically!"

In a small apartment with intimate walls

I strike a match.
Bliss, not a balcony on a May evening,
but a golden dome lit from within.

Apart of Me

At five, my daughter wrote her first pop song. She sang it to me once in a
        shy, whispery vibrato.
Here's "Apart of me" by Lydie Green:

you are apart of me
apart of me forever Forever oh yay
ou huh ou huh hmm hmm
yay

The poetry of apart as together. I think that's a great way to remind us
of all sorts of incongruities. & let us consider a girl's gradual awakening
        to what's inevitable.

A Final Poem

In this poem I am a father sitting
on the doorsteps
with the newspaper on an August morning.
The gnats, the moths, the light.
I'm going on reading
of a hundred things to occupy me
—then something that rips the cloth of day—

a man threw his four young children off a bridge.
There was a fight with his wife. He left.
Wherever he went, he went.
Then he came back, took the kids,
drove to the Dauphin Island bridge.
He stopped, got out.
I see them immovable in the back seat,

blind behind fogged glass.
The nature of obedience & love.
Each girl gripped him, embraced his neck.
Then a son.

The sun beams gladly on the steps of my home.
& in my mind the river flows—
there are days you can hear the mystery,
dark, always dark, something unseen
stealing each day.

While I sit with my little diary,
something dense
& tragic comes.

AFTER TIANANMEN SQUARE

More news in minor & major fugues,
so much terror.
A mother has been forbidden
to visit the spot in Tiananmen Square
where her son was killed.
Authorities aim a camera
at the spot to stop her from mourning there.
In shifts, police stare at that blank
of cement for hours, for years.
& what if she comes, unfolds herself
on the one spot she cannot,
looks into the bleak frame,
drums, tears & claws at the brick.
Imagine madness, sadness for all,
& the great shadow,
the stock of suffering.

Yet in the great desert of China,
you can almost smell the rain.
I see the vision of her son—
he stands straight up,
& in the bleak dim red light
tweaks a dream in his far-off eye.

THE PIPE BOMBER'S FINAL SUMMER NIGHT

I thought I'd heard a transformer blow.
But this morning my neighbor & his dog Buddha found a shirtless body at
       the park.
Legs folded underneath & the right arm gone.
There was nothing from the neck up, not even blood.
A pipe bomb had ignited in his hands.
The blast on the bark left a large rough navel. Heat spat him out,
his arm some distance to the tennis court.
His head erased, carried away.

It's beautiful here, a real Midwestern romance.
My wife steps out of a dress—she is the skin
of a river or grass in wind.
But the living are tragically living.
Life is like the crow screeching, "There is more than what you see."
A man might live like a heavy black bird
& like the Buddha said—
die a flash of lightning in a summer cloud.

A POEM TO COMPLIMENT CALLIE'S CLOTHES

Last night I was reading *The Anthologist* by Nicholson Baker. The narrator,
Paul Chowder, is an aging poet who's telling a class his best writing secret: "I
ask a simple question. I ask myself, 'What was the very best moment of your
day?'"

So I'm reading this thinking yes! yes! this is what I'll do, what we should do.
It's that simple. But as Chowder finishes his speech, the class looks at him. &
then he bursts into tears.

I admit my very best moment, walking the girls to school today,
is reason enough to live.

Here's what Callie wore (her clothes announce herself). I'll start from the
bottom up: neon green sneakers, orange laces, purple ankle socks, bicycle
shorts with rainbow-colored rings, a tank top with wider rings of rainbow, &
her black messenger bag bisected by a rainbow racing stripe.

How would our days be different if we wore rainbow rainbow rainbow?

A Woman Once Asked Carlos Castenada

how she can lead
a spiritual life.
He told her
every evening
she should sit down
& realize
that one day
her husband
and children
would die
in no particular
order & on
no particular day.

Each night,
my daughter
lays down her outfit
for the next day.
Tonight
a ribbon set high;
& below,
a cloud-colored shirt
arms wide;
two bracelets aloof

and a library book
for her right hand
to return;
black capris
above white
ankle socks,
toes out, comically.
My daughter,
a solitary girl
vanished, disappeared
into the floor.

SHE GROWS AN OAK TREE

On the radio, the old Irish poet discusses
the old Troubles, says the opposite of war
is not peace, but civilization.
He used to wish Belfast
was more like the rest of the world,
but now the rest of the world is like Belfast.
For civility, I defer to my daughter's hope,
her winter Science Fair promise
to grow an oak tree in our living room.
Her mind is full of sun, & her mood
is liberty-themed.
The pot is newly pregnant (she "changes its diaper"
every morning in the sink). She talks sweetly,
bathes it in plain, humble dirt.
And this skeleton lives! I can testify,
I can see even now—it keeps climbing, keeps climbing . . .
An infant in winter sun, reaching.

CROW POEM

Lately, just before waking, you say quietly, "Oh God. Oh God. Oh God."
Dread or adoration.
I leave you in bed, settle at the table to wait for a poem.

Our life is thin with poverty, the old spiral notebook & windows open.
Today, a crow flies up
lands on the pane & stares down, trying to read me—

then looks up into my eye like *I feel for you & I can't wait to leave,*
I'm nostalgic already for the fir trees & the moon,
& what is poetry even for?

THE FIRST WORD

Finally everything is white & silent. Very peaceful.
I'm absolutely alone & it's like a miracle.
Soon the kids will be up & I will be swamped.
Admittedly, I feel a bit funny
& hysterical for thinking of my own birth.

Only in a particular loneliness
does someone recall being born.
1965, a big March snow, my parents driving home.
They hit a white cast-off horse on a back country road.
After—the instant after—
my mother's body stuttered into labor.

Only now do I see
the astonished face of the riverbank, the horse who died
among the nearby trees & bushes & fresh beginnings of frost.
I am partly tucked in at the edges of the earth,
the white belly & neck of my mother,
her breast & slim crucifix,
& pointing beyond the snow
my father's hands trembling in the breath of morning
& my mother's voice telling us what to do next
& I woke up far away
falling into the river of day.

Ghost Poem

On the first day of my death
I would want to go back

what for
not solid earth

but the age of brightness
that bore the daughters

I want to sit
as if looking for work

when it is time
I follow the old dog

who is deaf and near blind
with the moon already

coming up
and the night passing

and the dog
feeling for the stairs

She stands for the moon
passing over its earth

leading me carefully
into the darkness.

Often I Do Not Drown

I was a young man on vacation in Hawaii with my family. But you know,
we're always finding things out—
it might be about dying or not, but no matter what,
something always happens. As it happens, my grandfather had served
            in Honolulu
in WWII. And there I was nearly forty years later, a tourist
waiting in the surf. I continued loafing, enjoying myself until a wave
ripped the swimsuit from my body . . .

A wave never gives respect. And so, for a time,
I closed my eyes as if to pray, "I'm done with my kind. I live alone."
I drifted as the clouds scudded seaward. I wanted beauty, not
the trouble of shore, disturbing the seaside town with my idiotic nakedness.

Weightless in the clear green medium, the penis is suppler than silk,
coiled in repose. Surrender, without navigation.
One can, by lack of effort, think like a wave,
at least in a partial degree.

I thought about a lot of different things, but none were straightforward.
To be undressed in the sea is to suddenly stir in some prenatal sleep.
            I could have called out,
but I looked around and saw only history—my aunt, uncle, brothers,
and parents, our bad relationships and cruelties. I almost felt persecuted.
My family there, pressing against each other pointing,
their concern purple as a bruise.

We're always at a critical point in history. I tend to sway darkly.
            I will always be alone.
& how to explain the ancient sea rising in my throat?

The ocean is just a melancholy man, and we're everything that's wrong.

Devotion

We drive down buried roads
and arrive at Frost's grave together
shoulders hunched, collars turned up.
One is never more dead than in Vermont in January.
The sun is frozen, locks the sky
to the hills; the snow is shadowed hard.
We are waiting with the wind.
Nevertheless, we are here to drink, squat
on our heels and wave to him.
Then Michael remembers his father is dead
and wishes Frost were here to minister something.
We improvise—the scotch and book of poems.
I read "The Wood-pile" too loudly
to the gathered snow. Vireos and bobolinks
bow on the dark branches; a simple cardinal,
the color of hot blood, holds
to the dogwood and is unalarmed.
What is a Frost poem for? Like the reflex of a star,
there's light in unsaying death, fame
in metaphors for spring
and liquor in a bird's name.

Old Death Again

My old dog
walks past the bird, comes to be let inside.
She knows, she knows day after day.
It is a knowing. It is not what you're told.

September Falling Everywhere

One rainy late afternoon,
Michigan Avenue—
rushing, attention
fixed, submissive head
down. Great stone and steel
monuments to upwardness
or the downed.
September falling everywhere,
and the going on.
Banks of bodies.
I walk south. Chicago
sags in a fall drizzle,
the old marshes buried
in the deeper city.
Everyone passes so fast,
the street beautiful
in its driving madness.
A single scrawny sparrow
falls real at my feet
down from a ledge
like a tossed rag.
In that moment,
from the sidewalk, innocently
looking up, the fully real memory
of the brother I neglect,
someone for whom
my guilt is a waiting bird,
its stillness
the formal love
erupting out of nowhere.

Mother on a Webcam Dances at *The Westerner*

Ladies Night, every Wednesday, I watch her.
Mom wears red, white, and turquoise.
She's seventy-three, and slides gracefully side by side by side
with Dorothy, Paula, and Nancy
(the husbands, so I've heard, are distant, brutal, or dead).

They dance in denim skirts above the knee.
Mom in her stars-and-stripes dress, silver boots with spurs,
grapevines on a sawdust floor.
The older ladies of Salt Lake City
turn in unison like birds in the sky.

I could pick up the phone, or buy a ticket and kiss her hello.
But I find that I don't.
From here in this chair, I feel somehow closer.
On my screen, she is entirely free of time.
She is there. And she is not there.
And all this happens in silence, no volume,
in the black-and-white of memory.

Mercy on mothers dancing in the light.

Mercy on her.

These Drunk Cities

Perhaps the world ends here, at an Al-Anon meeting on a Tuesday.
I'm the opposite of everyone who shares.
I'm the sullen boy who runs home
and wants to turn into dust.
When I think about my young father now, he's no longer
the stone man.
Everyone gets lost.

Elegist

after Mark Strand's "The Prediction"

In the middle of the day, I watched
my father watch his father die. Afterward,
under the boughs of the hospital's trees,
we were strangers in a poem, the sun beating
into it. That day the sun drifted over
the hospital to stay. Under the eaves
of the hospital, the absence of trees,
and for an instant, the future came to me:
sun falling on this hospital, on the windows
of his father's room. Sun falling on the lawns,
the doctors, the nurses, a man. I am
thinking of him thinking of him.
The sun drifting in. The sun streaming
into a man standing, thinking of death.

For Kenny at Sixteen

Friday nights at sixteen, a roomful of us. Our hard hearts and physiques.
And then there was Kenny who, when we'd leave, did what children
        are supposed to do—
he'd kiss his parents on the lips and say, "I love you."

We stood estranged, amazed. It was like seeing a unicorn jump through
        a rainbow!
When I left my house, I might throw a stone back at a window.
My people are repressive, choked—everything is saved
until someone dies, then we *might* emote in one enormous broken wave.

At the hospital, after Grandpa died, Dad and I never embraced
or exchanged love pledges—we shook hands.

Looking back, I see myself, only myself, driving home drunk in the dark
        on snowed roads.
I can picture my father pacing. The night is black, and dinner is cold
        on the stove.
My old man is waiting up worrying about my life,
and then, finally, turning out the light.

Donny Hid the Day

Death compels me. Interesting what is going through my mind now. Donny Dorton was born in 1965 a thin red-headed kid with a good heart and many other positive qualities that made him memorable for most of his short life, and the nuns from St. Anne's School were not there at his coffin because they knew the story, revelations of heaven denying him with no astonishment on saintly God's part—Donny, though, was pure, the mournful look of him, the hat-like shroud of red hair smoothed down his brow by the hand over blue serious eyes—I can deliver no better sermon, he was inexplicably full of sweetness—For the first twelve years of my life, while he lived, his brother routinely whipped him bloody, his mom kicked dog shit under their sofa, pity was his face but he was free of grief—Summers we'd lie on the earth, swap little dreams (I was told by adults to wake up to his no-good end, but children pay no attention, we are ghosts and don't see the dark valley when peace is gone and mercy too late and we play no more with whatever woe trails behind us like bad dreams).

Last Poem

Don't judge the rats.

We're all condemned.

Silent Poem

Just got back—
strange returning from the little house where I was raised.
I'm kind of stunned from it all.
Dad seemed too sad to look square in the eye.
We spent a few afternoons bored in the basement
where he once studied for the bar exam.
Those were the days he'd come from work, no time
to remove his long black overcoat before night school.
He sat wordless.
His office was a thick desk pushed into a corner.
Beside stacks of legal books,
across from where I played air hockey with my brother,
necktie loosened, eyes down,
he dreamed of the motorcycle he sold,
of any unfamiliar road,
and followed in his mind where it led past perfumed fields
and groves of mystery trees.
Our collie pups yelped, the paddles and puck clacked,
and eventually, like a sprung-lid,
he would explode,
and for a moment everything stopped
except the furnace's drunk talk. And Dad spoke to himself,
not words exactly, wiped his brow.
Then whimpers from the dogs, a new game began,
and sound slammed to the surface again.

Behold the man suffering in his dream.
Dear Dad, this poem sits softly down.
The silence is for you.

On the Day Spring Broke Out

On the day spring broke out
in the eighth year of her life,
Callie hums to herself then pipes up:
"When you want to kill yourself,
what you do is cut down, not across."
She holds up her arm, pulls back
her sleeve and shows me,
practicing with her finger.
Then in her little animal voice,
"Daddy, why would anyone
hurt themselves?" I start picking
through black glass, my mind unraveling.

Prodigal Daughter

You are always drumming your small fingers
and refusing to blink.
When you are mad this is a popular act:
write my name on a piece of paper, cross it out,
and hand it to me.

Once you said, "Santa Claus is not looking for you.
God is not looking for you."
I agreed.

I can even believe you exist to tease me
into writing about you.

You spend mornings looking out the window
for the cloud-white cat that patrols our yard each night,
and the killed baby rabbits always left
in the same spot. The cat does his work,
lays his report on our desk.

It is always a matter of life or death.

You are so serious about the predicament of nature.
You keep a field journal at five.
I ask if you write about the weather;
you look disbelieving as if I don't know a single thing.
You say, "It's for writing about animals
and their problems and when it's foggy what's blocking you."
Your first entry still feels true:
"The baby dolphin was lost in the woods of the sea."

There is something to be said for knowing that a house
is not the world.

As I wave in my young old age as if for the last time
watching you, I find my seat at the desk.
Unseen I stare back as you recede.

Death Again

Alone now, a lyric poet
in his unclean kitchen.
A sudden blast against window—
another bird mistakes glass
for sky and shrivels to the ground.
I ought to act. All I can do
is write, "Blood is cardinal-red,
as are the leaves,
and the vines that crawl."
Monster, I call myself.
I have no choice.
The fact is the dead bird
has a mate who moves gradually
from grass to branch to sky—
his way of asking,
What's the point of remembering
if it's followed by dying?
The scene reminds me of my mother
on the floor
after a midnight phone call—
her sister's death and Mom
like a corpse herself.
I pray without a prayer.
I want to fly out and away.
Did I really just say that?
Each moment is like this.

Reading for Ms. Doyle's First Grade Class

My daughter looks painfully proud, whispering
to her friends. Among the low smells and scrawls
of elementary school, the kids sit
in odd angles at my feet, look up

with much nose-picking and tittering.
Today, I don't read the greaved poems underlined
with suffering, but one set on the bright side
of the moon, another with undead birds

flocking over a tire store, a rant about the pain
in my shoulder, a Big Bang pantoum,
and my hopeful ode to folding a napkin.
Question-and-answer time. A long silence

hovers over the packed classroom.
I start to panic . . . I lean forward and ask,
"What is poetry?" Instantly, I see the truth
in their faces. They ponder

the arcana of another adult.
I look over to see Lydie's worried face.
She teaches me about difficulty. A poem
is a classroom that contains my daughter,

the molding world map, math games with X times
and repeated Y's, hand-made
planets, and the nearness
of the alphabet. On a good day, poetry's

dry silence surprises.
So it is that finally, Caleb,
the bad boy with an unpained face asks,
"Can you tie my shoe?" And I do.

Looking at a Tulip with Lydie

Enjoying the not yet summer,
we cut a tulip from the yard—
"The swizzlestick at the center
is a stamen . . . a penis," I say.
And like the idiot statesman
of pollination, I continue—
"There are ovaries too, somewhere."
Luckily, she does not argue.
It is a hot day. Everything
is quiet and peaceful except now
there's the idea of a flower
and a bee . . . doing things.
I grow old watching her
in the garden.
The elements of her mother—
the same hair,
the responding beauty in her face.
Can one discuss a young daughter
with so much misery around?
Brecht said yes.
So, beside our dirty white garage,
we come to a new understanding
of the lily family.

Flower Masterpeace

This is spring.
Believe me
this is your season, Callie.

Lately, you've been drawing flowers.
Today, a carnation?
You begin.
A central petal,
which multiplies in all directions.
You call it, "Flower Masterpeace."
You, you, you
wild, and with flower, upward.

But there is something new
on your mind,
something inward,
Callie.
Lately, each morning,
you present yourself
conscious of your hair,
your dress,
the slope of your shoulders.
You are transformation.
You are on the brink.
Days you will be wounded to the heart.

This is your drawing.
This drawing is you, Callie.
It's time we make it clear.

Anniversary

I was a lost soul
married in the desert.

Her face, what comes
when the wind warms and rains.

Diamond

after Hayden Carruth

I know a nice man who makes diamonds
from human ash (owns the patent).
It's all perfectly normal for him
to leave the house in the morning,
maybe in green hazy springtime, and he passes
the daffodils yellow by the fences
and before him on his desk
the remains of a life. Who needs the old names
for death? He speaks
in flame as he works to transform grief,
work it down
into something other than darkness.

And listen: when I'm lost,
what a waste of your best sunny days, my dear,
to visit a grave by the back of the cemetery. You,
who are entirely loving and rare, deserve
finally a husband
who will accent your yellow silk dress, the one
where you glow like a new moon.
In those drifting moments
when you know me only as light (not this scrap of a poem). I,
in my bright shining eye,
will look back with death's
flawless clarity.

The League of Mercy

Poetry is answering a wrong number with *Yes*. So
when the distressed young man called to ask,

"Is this the League of Mercy?" like a child, I said *No*,
but then logically, I handed the phone to you.

Lexa, in every possible way, you are sincere. You
listen when most are passive or unaware,

your presence a form of public dearness.
He told of his mind and its agony. Over time

in the bedroom air, the opus of his past came clear—
he was molested by someone he loved. No metaphor

parses the ground that is bottomless. He was teetering,
taking sleeping pills. His story blew up like a full moon.

I lay in the dark light and looked out our window
at the cold sky. As if speaking to let the hope creak in,

you said finally, "Wait. I am here."
Once a poem, I tend to name the garden I live in.

In this service, I'm advised to brood on our small rental,
remember again, and listen.

On Being a Tiger in California

Tatiana was brought to the San Francisco Zoo to provide an old Siberian tiger, Tony, with a wife. They talked of the place as their own. Their barren rocks were faux stone and formed an unbeautiful island surrounded by a moat. They loved to lie and look for meanings in the hundred thousand flaws of the gleaming city. Theirs was recognition without sound, a lingering dream of not answering to a name. Then Tony died of cancer of the spleen. He was buried somewhere far. Afterward, Tatiana was known for roaring alone into the dark.

One night, after hours, three stoned and drunk young men left their BMW in the parking lot and began a slow creep through the zoo. They did not stand and sing to the lion but hurled stark insults and sticks . . . stumbling on they spat at the camel and they declared war on Tatiana—whirled pine cones and stones into her dark. They interrupted her dream (she liked to be unseen and track the moon's rising and know it all through the night).

Of course rich boys like to taunt, especially when mammals are at a disadvantage, held down, arms pinned, etc. Imagine them sniggering, strutting away like gold medal winners in the Little Arrogant Prick Olympics . . . they turn a corner and in what must have been an unhysterical man-caught-in-a-dilemma-he-cannot-understand kind of scene—Tatiana was standing there, waiting.

Here was the raw moment. The color and size and hunger unseen until what is undoubted can't be doubted. Believing comes after. In her decency, she killed one right off. To the other two, she promised intimate revenges: Shakespeare's *terrors of the earth*.

Of course time was running out. Before long, Tatiana was shot. Eventually for evidence, the authorities removed her head, tail, and paws (humans being stone cowards at heart). It's said a sympathetic sculptor made a statue of Tatiana hidden somewhere in the San Francisco foothills. Art followed her there into the thickets, followed her calls.

And like the silence at the end of every story, no one knows how she escaped. Somebody made threats, the challenge, the smug face-off. The Dark was deeply wronged. And she tracked them—they stunk like ruined movie stars, like San Francisco's jacked up prices. I don't believe in revenge but in the loneliness of a tiger who harbors a grudge against the hopeless and their bright valley.

America

after Robert Creeley

Old Foreclosure Artist. How strange
to sell eternity to unwealthy customers.

The stars over the sprawling
meadowland bordered by factories

from Chicago to Flint to Moline.
Old Allegory, sentence

and guard, you laugh at the miracle,
poke the arctic ice, laugh your smoke.

Old Oldsmobile beyond our power
to carry. *America,*

you ode for reality! Look around.
The large families of the poor.

There's not much point confessing
to things. We love the sound of gunfire.

Everywhere West
(The All-Purpose American Road Song)

for Mark Neumann

Before us nothing but speed. From old AZ
the whole loneliness of the Southwest
builds a bright twilight and the great tangled
road where the sea used to be
is terribly shaky country running down
and down. We've been driving
from then to now
when the sun is hot on the blacktop
and the radio plays everything
like a busy main street onward into the night.
Seeing this you finally know daydreams
or afternoons are casual mysteries
like traffic dancing in early dawn—
or the picture of sky always sky
like the sea with sun coming in a holy
visual entirety. Roadside scrubbery
and the mock sleep of a little town.
Arizona's loneliness as the evening
darkness comes on, visions of sand and raw
buttes, a man dropped off without a word
on a country road, the desert night
torn down, snoring, low—The world is loaded,
long shot looks and the great harvest of souls
shaken loose across the country—
Under a used sun, the absence of anything
will do, the openings of space in Santa Fe—
The house back in the hills shows a light
no bigger than a star, the huddled cactus lands
and the vision of a rented Sky City moon—
Looking for home is this dream in the air
that nobody is going to touch,
a silence standing upright in the wind—
and the tattooed guy sleeping at the gas station
in Gallup (What a rough night!)
with no dreams at all,
or else a dream that may or may not

teem with new skies—I see rabbits
loose in the sparse grass—
There beside the roadway an empty
Dewar's bottle thrown into a pond of creosote
("At the bottom of the cliff
America is over and done with" says James Wright)
(an owl rises from a dark place at an indecent hour),
in St. Louis the moon grows heavy, silvery
(What is the moon doing in St. Louis?)—
We are herded, not driven, like busted up
black clouds dreaming of fantastic violence—
I hear people say "Oh where are the Arapaho?"
they sit and stare in drugstores the rainbow trout
mounted on a wall next to the calendar
picture of a sky-reflecting lake—
The retired buffalo in Oklahoma
stare for hours into far off mountains—
their faces don't criticize or editorialize
but there is distance in their American-ness . . .
Now comes the great poet—
Whitman—a single voice leaving a blue space
where the old stood before—
"O a word to clear one's path ahead endlessly!
O something ecstatic and undemonstrable! O music wild!"
Now, the motor whines and the country splinters.
This is the poem of terminal life,
a lullaby of grimy machinery
or the beauty of driving.
We'd all like to pass by in a 1995 Cadillac
is what Bukowski meant, sliding around
on the highway headed inexorably in a big car
out of control. The world will forget us anyway.
America goes on—the long throat of the Mississippi
lost between the turnpike and the lawyers' signs
looming among the locust trees, toward
some dark church below the chemical hills
somewhere between sand shoals and the tottering
palaces of dismantled fairgrounds—
here, the poplar trees are white hair, the front porches
vaguely stunned and drunk bent over
with gray mysterious detail—
The long road, the slow dusk, the gallop,

the new wheat, the drowning out, the quick sundown—
the huge and swollen darkness of Elkhart,
this loneliness business, the glare of bare fields
and the evening eagle, the private miles
and floating road—the long hard rest of the world,
everyone and everything:
the miles down motorama we are going going
blurred beings in uncrashed cars around the bend
toward horizon, the geese swollen with love
in dark furrows, dark crickets in the plowed up
borderland. From here to Streetsboro
along this flat universe this corridor
of willows, bus windows, good families
and a little spider tracing in the wind—
climb, hitch a ride beyond the bravest truck
on Route 14, cast your cloud, don't be dead,
write high, lift your kind even as it rains—
the crazed lone eager road ahead. Here,
a greeting to my country and a quick complaining,
US is going to hell with all the eternal
progress, withered shopping malls,
cemeterial steel mills and no black-and-white Holsteins—
dark water clouds search and gaze down
at modest corn grain, the secrets of wheat
stored like unnamed poor, time stretches
in the lonely leanings of telephone poles,
the distance and promise of the Hudson.
Where are we now? This America
of surface—and life as tremendous
heavyweight car, what else?— speckled with rust,
less white than snow—drifts in a cool evening
in a cold dream—death a tiny smoke-haze
across trees, radiant silence on wet asphalt—
Heavy night and low under starlight,
what are we going to do?—All we can do
is drive afraid to call our mother who is dying,
come on come on home, eat the apples, wait out—
Mother is sleeping like a river,
Mother belly down in the cold autumn thorns—
We are windy unlit alone in the night hours,
Mother cold, Mother darkness—her life like

a blue secret smoothed over, the road soothes where it goes.
Appearing out of nowhere, out of pine trees—
The self is the beginning of red pines
in low mountains, the road's heart is innocent
and we are rejected by nothing—
Fold around us soft black earth burning oaks
and moon breaking through in bright darkness.
This eastern ghost place, the small folds, dark yellows,
the understanding of grass, of the field like the flatcar
of a freight train, the bird on the branch—
twilight comes flowing past—
the marble-colored clouds kindhearted
one here and there, everything
that was once far.
The end is a picture of country
in rainy light: the white-haired boards of the barn,
the sumac tree opens its brindle buds
and suddenly the wanderer—
He emerges from his shell
like water from the mountains. Wherever home is,
it lies beside him unguarded in the clear.

Making America

A liger: half lonely lion,
half horny tiger. Stuffed,
with a snarl of course,
for there's nothing lonelier
than a liger. Homely lion
or uglier tiger, coat of furry
sun and sorry stripes.

A Particle of Dread

in memory of Sam Shepard

During the Q & A, it's clear nothing can change him.
He goes it alone. His frozen glances and proud artist's cleft.
His last response: "I'm no spokesman for the West."
What I remember is Lexa hurrying backstage.
Sam Shepard against a wall. She says, "Hi, we're from the West!"
His response is a little poem: "Oh."
And then what happens? Jessica Lange opens a door.
When you see her, you stand up suddenly straighter.
Your eyes are wide. Her prettiness is intimate, out of place.
What happens next? We wait. We outwait, let them feel our presence.
Then Jessica asks if we'd like to go to dinner.
We find ourselves walking through SoHo.
Occasionally, Jessica's face flowers into a smile.
Sam's eyes are splintery ice. Eventually, we find a place.
Jessica and Lexa arrange themselves at a table. Sam and I
stay at the bar. We order a bottle of Hornitos Tequila
and the clouds disappear. His excessive aloneness
and silence cut loose. He burns all night. Talks
his ideas to the bone. His hunger spreads
to the brunette bartender. Then, everything grinds down—
Jessica enters, slaps him hard. (She and Lexa exit.)
Sam jangles his body with all its sadness,
"My life is falling apart. I can see it.
My next play is titled after a line from Oedipus Rex:
'a particle of dread.'" A woman enters, crosses the restaurant,
falls on her knees at our feet. She says she needs money
to buy medicine for her daughter. It's a long speech
about ex-husbands and hospitals, bus fairs and pharmaceuticals.
(In his plays, women are mothers who walk in at the end,
vehicles for sex or children or a free meal.)
She says she'll show us her breasts. Before we can say no or yes,
she does. Sam hands her fifty bucks.

Inventing the Dolphin

In a blue-painted pool sponsored by Corona and Sol,
It's hard to see the larger ocean. Picture a lonely dolphin
Waiting to get paid. His forced smile, his blow hole opening
For coins. They call him Chuy, a Mexican nickname for Jesus.
He takes his fish lazily from the trainer, and you know,
If he could walk backwards from here to the sea, he would.
We are his 2:30.

Standing in life vests, all grouped in the shallow end like Baptists,
We're told to stroke him, but carefully. We're warned to avoid
His pinhole ears that hear what we cannot, also his blowhole,
A second mouth that speaks an ocean tongue of shrieks and clicks.
I can see by the trainer's caution, our innocence is dangerous.
He says if Chuy takes a hand in his mouth, sometimes he's curious,
We should not pull, but let him release us. Also, it's a myth
Dolphins push drowning swimmers to shore. To a dolphin,
All humans look to be drowning. Besides, their instinct would be
To push us out to sea, to safety.

Looking close, I see in his wet grey eyes a child's knowing buoyancy.
I feel an intimacy, like he might turn to me in some small café and say,
"I think there is something you should know."
He's not as slippery as I thought. And his skin, just like the moon
Shining back, that still silver, is cool to the touch, the exact temperature
Of the water. We take turns in a strange communion touching
His forehead, laying small bloodless fish on a big blue tongue.
We are educated people, but I sense among us a competition
For whom Chuy likes best. We command cheap tricks and he jumps—
First circling, gaining inhuman momentum. He fears for his job.
He works. His back bent as to a desk holding his breath.

Suddenly he leaps—pure muscle, no bones—Jesus the way we wish him
To be, nosing a blue-green ball, his fins not quite fingers or feet.

From Childhood

for Richard Jones

There was church before school—this would have been
forty years ago—inside all were alone,
a small crowd of widows and widowers.
Their own children grown far out into the world.

I sat at the back. Last pew. Head down
in sleep or waking to homework. Outside was cold.
I remember their mumbled prayers far off
in that enormous space, the drift of incense
as if from a monastery garden.

In those early hours of my being, I was free
of holy feelings until the end,
when those thin and bleached mothers and fathers
paused their leaving to reach down, touch my hair,
and bless my timid growing and fear.

After the Dragonflies

Dear Brother,
remember the day I said

I saw a dead body?
I count the lies.

You ran and ran, terrified,
up a hill. I followed

through the dead grass, until we
climbed out into dragonflies!—

hundreds shaped a whirlwind around
you, an embrace and a warning.

This habit of memory.
I refused to love you once. You,

my principal witness. Our otherness
mirrored in those insects who see

everywhere at once. One feels confined
sifting old summers for clues.

I cannot know you. It is the normal way.
The concentrics of growing up. Death

itself has been building, and forgetfulness.
I have been rearranging.

Lately, I've been opening deep drawers.
Things have come to that.

The Two Sides of the River

The time I said to my mother, "There's no God.
There's not." She was hoping there was, wished
to see her dead parents again in heaven, her two dead
brothers and sister. She asked if I was sure.
I held to it, a small man miniscule in my innocence.
Mother of love and loneliness, I am falling eyes shut.
Today, I pray to you for all the oblivion to come.

What to Read

History continues in the intricately
cut news clippings my mother mails
stuffed in a single envelope—
the periodic revelations of ex-flames
broke, collapsed, or cleared away.
Never the Pope declaring peace,
but the blank abundance of those
once sensual girls now transitory
and obscure, like my mother herself
in her shredded time and cluttered room
cutting out pieces of my life.

The Whole Story

after Eavan Boland

A mother deer and child fawn lying here in the yard
As if we're all suddenly somewhere else.
They are too close to the road.
I go as near as I dare,
Find the courage to reach slowly down.
Unafraid, the deer-child rises to console me.
It's what a daughter can give.
She is a source. Language can't make her.
In the end, I am nothing more.

The Self-Conscious Clock

Age nine, my daughter surprised me by writing a story called "The Self-Conscious Clock." She looked up and said her teacher didn't like it.

I stepped back. "I didn't know you were writing." She said, "It's about a clock who hates being looked at, so he's trying to stop time. Oh, Dad, it's been hard."

I kissed her head. Already, she hangs at the edge, crossing her arms. She watches the day visible around her, watches sparrows climb toward the distant clouds, watches the black head of the dog laze. In her mind, time is battering the surface of the earth, the world as broken animal hiding its face.

A few days ago, I asked if she solved the plot. She said, "The clock scratched his own guts out. All humans were screaming and crazy. Then one brave little girl gave him more numbers. The end."

Notes

p.11 "A Vision of Now" is the title of a poem by Hayden Carruth.

p. 19 "Thanks" was inspired by W.S. Merwin's "Thanks."

p. 33 The title, "September Falling Everywhere" adapts a phrase from Desmond Egan's poem, "Through Flurries of Wind and the Rain."

p. 34 The end of "My Mother on a Webcam Dances at *The Westerner*" echoes the last two lines of James Wright's "Dawn near an Old Battlefield, in a Time of Peace": "Mercy on the pure Yonne washing his face in the water. / Mercy on me."

p. 35 In "These Drunk Cities," the first phrase, "Perhaps the world ends here" adapts the title of a poem by Joy Harjo.

p. 52 "Everywhere West" is the text to a poem-film featuring a compressed 8-minute video made by Mark Neumann of a cross-country drive from Flagstaff, Arizona to Bucksport, Maine. The film can be seen at *chrisgreenpoetry.com*.

p. 64 "The Self-Conscious Clock" was inspired by Mark Strand's "Translation."

About the Author

Chris Green is the author of four books of poetry: *The Sky Over Walgreens*, *Epiphany School*, *Résumé*, and *Everywhere West*. His poetry has appeared in such publications as *Poetry*, *The New York Times*, *Court Green*, *Prairie Schooner*, and *Columbia Poetry Review*. He's edited four anthologies including *I Remember: Chicago Veterans of War* and the forthcoming *Poetic Justice: A Poem by 100 Chicago Poets on Gun Violence* (Big Shoulders Books, 2020). He also started the Poetic Justice League, a forum for collaborative political poetry: *thepoeticjusticele.wixsite.com*. He teaches in the English Department at DePaul University. More information can be found at *chrisgreenpoetry.com*.

Other Recent Titles from Mayapple Press:

Terry Blackhawk, *One Less River*, 2019
        Paper, 78pp, $16.95 plus s&h
        ISBN 978-1-936419-89-0
Ellen Cole, *Notes from the Dry Country, 2019*
        Paper, 88pp, $16.95 plus s&h
        ISBN 978-1-936419-87-6
Monica Wendel, *English Kills and other poems*
        Paper, 70pp, $15.95 plus s&h
        ISBN 978-1-936419-84-5
Charles Rafferty, *Something an Atheist Might Bring Up at a Cocktail Party*, 2018
        Paper, 40pp, $14.95 plus s&h
        ISBN 978-1-936419-83-8
David Lunde, *Absolute Zero*, 2018
        Paper, 82pp, $16.95 plus s&h
        ISBN 978-1-936419-80-7
Jan Minich, *Wild Roses*, 2017
        Paper, 100pp, $16.95 plus s&h
        ISBN 978-1-936419-77-7
John Palen, *Distant Music*, 2017
        Paper, 74pp, $15.95 plus s&h
        ISBN 978-1-936419-74-6
Eleanor Lerman, *The Stargazer's Embassy*, 2017
        Paper, 310pp, $18.95 plus s&h
        ISBN 978-936419-73-9
Dicko King, *Bird Years*, 2017
        Paper, 80pp, $14.95 plus s&h
        ISBN 978-936419-69-2
Eugenia Toledo, tr. Carolyne Wright, *Map Traces, Blood Traces /
        Trazas de Mapas, Trazas de Sangre*, 2017
        Paper, 138pp, $16.95 plus s&h
        ISBN 978-936419-60-9
Eric Torgersen, *In Which We See Our Selves: American Ghazals*, 2017
        Paper, 44pp, $14.95 plus s&h
        ISBN 978-936419-72-2
Toni Ortner, *A White Page Demands Its Letters*, 2016
        Paper, 40pp, $14.95 plus s&h
        ISBN 978-936419-70-8

For a complete catalog of Mayapple Press publications, please visit our website
at www.mayapplepress.com. Books can be ordered direct from our website with
secure on-line payment using PayPal, or by mail (check or money order). Or order
through your local bookseller.